A MOTIVE FOR DISAPPEARANCE

RAY RAGOSTA

A Motive for Disappearance

Burning Deck/Anyart, Providence

ACKNOWLEDGMENTS:

Some of these poems first appeared in *Apex of the M, Aufgabe, Denver Quarterly, Hambone, New American Writing* and *Untitled: a Magazine of Prose Poetry.*

Burning Deck is the literature program of Anyart: Contemporary Arts Center, a tax-exempt (501c3), non-profit organization.

The cover reproduces a collage by Keith Waldrop

ISBN13 978-1-936194-15-5 original paperback

for my wife, Geraldine

CONTENTS

PARTNER TO US ALL

Four Signs

A dream of three cities which vanish,

and where pines bend with good intention,

... prescribes countermeasure.

Four signs point to the error of ways:

egregious flight,
polished air in heat,
tempered sleep,
a meeting in the garden of tongues.

Split

Tribe tempers compunction.
Bird's edge crops their stare.
Horns saturate music,
squawks and highs hitting the fringe of earshot.

Enigmas sprout from their soil.

Blood element of abstraction
lines a shining interior.

Their tales, a perfect infection of memory.

*

Lame speak offshoot.
Energy pours from wounds.
No use trying to make sense of it,
for unknown is the preoccupation,
in the mirror looking out.

Shift interposes — easily.
Some are talking;
others pace, in time, the measure of ways.

Occasionally one in dark sinister dress
holds a candle. No one approaches.

*

In the garden a man dances
beauty to the untrained eye,
in stages.
A dumb look on his face,
he is not the one they thought he was.

There is a vexing sensation,
a question, then a syllable

that lingers.

Split marked with X hangs there
as white light cryptogram.

Done Deal

Done deal at the circumference —
outsiders rig the scene.
A drifter signals "Tell me
another day passes
in absentia …

another turn
on a blind planet."

At this hour a light in the window
is bright with suggestion,
framed in aged wood,
paint curled like winter leaves.

Silence leaves a depression there.

*

We have cleared the place of obstacles.
Small sounds fish out a recurring dream.

Subterranean blue spot indicates
a true north somewhere
we cannot visualize,

and some parts played out on our time
twist through an older scene.

It moves farther off. I breathe in.

*

A whisper in the keys
relates to mind going blank.

Orbit traces
a moving territory as home.

The arena of possibility
becomes more narrowly defined.

*All those people downstairs
from up here seem to buzz
collectively like insects,*

who continually repeat
a dance of diagonals in a room.

*

Stung possibility as sidekick,

we land face down
on foreign soil,

pictures of a lost capital passing
before our eyes.

*Return is calculated on the wing
in a hollow where nocturnal sessions
spawn series of madcap endings.*

There are depressions in the landscape
three digits deep, which form a pattern
that looks lived in.

*

The start and stop music plays
on this side of the equation
whose other half is half gone.

Habitation groans under the strain.

The determining agent is reversal of expectation:
Improvisation on the negative term.

Residual accompaniment far left.

Now This Move

Mood grows indigenous and centripetal,
blends then targets
where partner to us all lives.

An ill-defined gravity swings us here,
swings us there.

Closing ranks, we still fail
to achieve high ground.

"So what's the contention?"
quotes a deaf man,
who wanders a geometry
that once was a room.

*

Past navigates possibility;
all details are counted in,
but to find a recorder
with that kind of attention span …
may as well structure
accord's final leap.

Something outside wails
among the stars.

It is evidence of itself —

mode that obviates act:
its own equilibrium.

*

A tree standing leafless in the muddle
is the only population.
Our house is filled with cobwebs
and ghosts of visitors — nonetheless contagious.

Over time we get used to cracks in the wall
and achieve steady-state — of mind.
Threats lessen. Blows more readily glance off.

Out on the point landscape changes rapidly,
like geology under a microscope.

Glass darkens. The obverse gets more obscure.

Whoever arrives bears a violet aura.
We join with them, touching at the kneecaps,
then break off, as in some kind of dance
that feels otherworldly but is not.

*

Doubling of fracture
opens distance between;

reaches empirical overload.

The crush of circumstance quickens.

Flowers line pathways to the possible.

Alternatives are closer than they appear:

A mirror reduces their size,
marking a rupture in wave.

*

The circle is broken, not as the song says;
is an anomaly stretched out
 — and in its timeline we read
temptations of a tribe born on the skids.

The edge of the glass is sharp,
but its center loses clarity
and measure slides
"fold according to fold."

An image comes into focus,
revealing twelve small ciphers
concealed within.

We have journeyed alongside,
observed when feasible,
to find the way forever runs parallel.

*

Repetition forces arrangement.
We are directed to plead a new cause.
No longer did it seem possible,
yet others kept insisting.

"Fingers grew weak from trying to hold on
as we sped through undercurrents,
undetected, hidden by power of darkness.

Our words fell into silent passage."

There are four corners, all with the same angle,
and other possibilities, too,
all of them outside this place.

Some of the wall is fallen.
The city is no longer our destination;

but a foil to our real desire.

AFTER IT ALL

Twenty-First

From makeshift bunkers
we view our last days,

former lineage
now vague.

Disjointed scouts we wander
a cold stretch through rocky terrain

— case on venture
is closed,

for Greywater Grandfather,
tall tales in absentia,
insists on clowning around.

Three Figures

A devil stands in the background
absorbing the strangest blue light from the field.
It's a jungle out there and beauty
is carried in different proportions.
It's not the breath of foul air
that scatters us toward four points of the compass,
each corresponding to a different season.

So why is everyone in that corner reaching up?
Any goal is out of the frame.
Memory can't recover details,
except, perhaps, a tree ascending somewhere.

We have fallen as three figures
stunned by a beguiling symmetry,
its haunting configuration a near miss
linked to some others' part.

This way, that way we no longer recognize.

Official North

The dead end is up.

The sky grays and your touch
is always your touch,
a little sweaty
but it still sends me into reverse.

That's the whole deal now.

I have inherited the look of the lost
from my father's side.

There he is sitting alone
at the banquet table
dreaming of a return in disguise.

It's only a picture. I know.
But that's him — in my dream.

The Unexpected

Pulled toward
an awkward register

(face imprinted in sand)

so what impression there is

is discontinuous.

Ballast reverts

and leaves us edging along
a treacherous curve,

where there is no recovery.

A smaller costume is offered.

Bundled on the sly,
it feels just the right size.

Non-Narrative

Deep scar divides
boon sinister
and hides

the domain
exculpated

(it must be some other cause).

Frame without luster
dribbles it away

a motion, a candle,
neither affects the other

a moment, a monument,
neither stands on two legs

Fringe

The feed is polar cropped down,
blended by crosswind …
frigid tone from a voice in the wings.

The old man is strapped upright in his chair,
his eyes shooting blanks.

No terms hold him accountable now.

We investigate his past in a land
where it snows occasionally,
but more often the horizon has a look of scorn.

A sign appears, cut from another dream.

He will be restored to a peaceful kingdom,
where, it appears, there is no way out.

Against Margin

Violent up against margin.

Compulsion turns to adage,
or squinty reverence,

detected leagues below surface

… arrives in waves,

drifts "in radiance."

Repetition of three distinct figures

on three different days.

Sign which "acts that way."

There's a convoy of the banished.

Now sighted.

A string of loss winds through
where nocturne folds into horizon.

And light's neuter.

Signs: Speaking

Backslide of consequence
swings vertical,

"color and motion taken away."

Epilepsy of courage diminishes

and no justice comes
from the stern look of the lost,

by which alternatives are discussed
hours on end

(only alternatives).

Contiguous, in incomprehension.

Sinking Hymn

The sinking hymn lingers …
as vocables in undertow,

later read as scars upon the body.

This screen — credence of event
farther off than sense —
is sustained at the curve,

where lineage goes undivulged.

Observers now are self-described
as "at table, on edge,"
through duration of leisure
and investigations of
superannuated time.

Implant of immediate flares on-site,

dirge-like moment
held length of breath.

PAST RETURNS

Valentine From G

A flawed sex
and viewpoint

(I grow to love the
always warm pelt)

The play of desire

calculated

image and likeness
and the stuff of life.

Reflection in the Strange Waters
That Run Beneath the Old Bridge

Hard estrangement flakes off surface,
discontent "kicking up dust"
blown across continents,

… moves toward us.

Cold creeps through (as sole touches stone),
despite tempering effect of light.

The "winding path,
not level, not steep"
enters through
a former recension,

structure altered further,
heavily annotated

with scenes of stray angels
carved in relief
along arches,

drifting descriptions I'd mull over,

neither at the beginning
nor to the point of it all.

Just impeded stance
in measured heat
of split intention.

*

Partaking substances
in the glow turn gray,

assumed negation
desiccated.

Her appearance at the bridge
re-assesses pulse,

collides with stray proposal,

at proportioned speed.

Space gone to
brilliant tandem arrangement.

*

Function halts in the solemn mode —
black patch slung across,
like answer in a vulgar tongue.

"And write these things,
that they seem spoken
by a third person.

As 'Excrements of an aged mind.'"

Medium is found
to float parallel,
somewhere beyond the object
of attraction we've assembled,

who operates "in them through others."

Further "screen for so much love on my part."

Decades are reduced now,
to an irksome trace,

pearl built up from
history of such commotion.

*

What is this dual substance driving at?
But fierce polarity of temperament
in habitable zones
and their extremes

("... the wound it gives
cannot be healed by herbs ...").

Impatience of "indeterminate character."

At distant corners
more than wires are being crossed,
as the whole sanctuary
verges on explosion.

Peripheral conjecture
plummets down the slope,
triggering avalanche.

Debris turns in on itself,
without coming to conclusion:

more false leads
to contaminate phenomenology,

another bad turn in the narrative
of fits and starts,

failing to flush out daily accretion.

Everything turns "fluid cold";
barely moving tongues grow
distanced from thought.

*

Submerged extension
of Tunisia,
at night, descends;

puts the brakes on speech
in flames, behind screens

— removal to a zero point,

where the curtained portrait
holds its trident clues
(inverted) as signposts.

The unforeseen stare
(a cooked stronghold)
slips down all suspicion.

*

Some odd genetic equipment
generates a string of command
triggering "sore change … in aspect,"
like bitter prospect bronzed
concealed in the park
despite traffic and dancing.

"A corruption produced by
individual contribution."

Or total eclipse of orientation
groomed for a "puzzled brow";

wit tending toward cancellation.

Lately I've found myself
"vexed and impeded"
from this "greedy appetite
for things new and unknown."

Feeling it paper-thin
and drying in the wind

— lost moment stuck in branches,
without song.

*

Concordance in blue,
note bends to its quiver,

emotional center,
circumscribed,

left on edge.

Her repute grows
like the hue of grass

(a seasonal occurrence)

and supplants expression.

Cipher drifts back
into the opening to speak.

Her face,
beneath burden,

"revolving to its own note."

*

On the scale of unexpected ruin,
we grow blind to it,

the invitation is misread
for its allure,

vehicle vanished
into the core.

Hard saying, overgrown, crumbles.

Her effect, by slow increments,
moves inward.

*

Yet I cannot come to assign
the deed of serenity
to one adored as congruous
and asleep in greater diversion.

Not so with the remaining lineage

(beneath hot tears streaming).

With a slight move of the plectrum,
we elucidate fitfully
a prevailing scorn
moving in across dark waters.

*(A figure huddles in the corner
clinging to the cask
dampness up to his knees.)*

Lesson gained from inward veneration
tuned by derangement — without remorse.

Portrait

Panel One

Synthetic pain shoots through — broken nose,
colossal Inquisition, excessive allure —
the straight line is not what we've come to know,

harassed out of a conformable element,
sensation of red, air elastic (neither shared).

Three columns of pleading describe our fresco
and indicate a broader swatch cut from the heart,
price for dalliance sown piecemeal —

incongruous in space,
cocked slightly toward "scene in red,"

which doesn't migrate into the faculty
of representation, named rival,
"not departed from the vulgar view."

Medallion One

Mummified in an ice-storm,
he passed young and in retrograde,
age before his time,

then was left for the extended holiday.

Stone placed over the eye conceals
an unknown which wells up there each night,
demanding unswerving tension

— No more than a finger in the sludge
to skin the wound over.

Medallion Two

Expansion sunk in private
is not prime yet rises
to the occasion blind,

inference watered down,
a jewel in the side,
dark side,
grown chameleon in treatise.

Panel Two

The cartoon's proboscis,
angled authoritarian, inquires
after the impressionable.

"Dangerous postures are worked in, with
windings and turnings of a bulky body,
… his handiwork unmistakable …"

Jottings are then made, notes taken down;
a testament formalized.

The cartoon's proboscis introduces
a variation on itself —
"bird on a wire" staring into a window,

where it observes an intense grilling,
which it fails to understand
due to the structure of its blindness.

Intensity grows within,
until the bird bursts into flame.

Residue drifts on idle wind,
finally coming to rest
on its beam of atonement.

Medallion Three

Misgiving leads to more plausible
willingness "absolutely denied,"
for sensuous elements
are summed in obverse,

"...showered with cornmeal
to make them look like clowns."

Though nothing comes of their
blooming into aggressive subspecies,
who follow a different clock
while talent grows Westward in heat,

the "here spoken of,"
I self-contradictory.

Epigrammatic terror hits in small doses.
Figure is inflated beyond a stare
 — simple difference
navigated by climactic order.

Panel Three

Providence had it miscarried;
and it was born in an intermediary sphere
 — geometer's space fragile,
within a tighter circle,
as if conveyed upon thorns.

We find ourselves navigating obscure streets,
same incomprehensible
business of sense
that weighs both representations,
contracted into semblance
caught in the wrong light
 — a flash in its Southern quarter.

Diluted insight
remains remarkable in its rigor,
as if inscribed,

for the more stubborn heart is assembled,
amply grounded 'on the sleeve'
and shown aggregate.

Community of reference,
viewed in meditation,
slits the scroll crosswise.

Medallion Four

Space is nothing
but sensibility
mobilized for the occasion,

reciprocal attraction diffuse
along the same fixed points.

The necessary separation
had never been made —

Basement coolness
slows extraction at each point.

Medallion Five

It's day; there is no day man,
for his categories are found defective.

As there is red and a circle,
then a red circle

which fades with
stain of disruptive inquiry.

PLAIN

Other

The border between them and us
is reduced to singular,

afterthought
in a photograph alive
with a pulse heading West.

Purpose is closed
as it has always been

— scar that crosses
what is drawn
to its own sphere.

Exit

Tall order is reborn
as adversary,

tides of change
spit back up.

Lines encircle a smaller depiction —
something no human can get a stick on.

Even "close call" gets a name

and flattens objects on its horizon.

Enclosure

A voice tells me,
"You are playing at the borders,

straying into other fields."

A cocoon grows around
and I inherit its living edges.

One pulse throbs into the next.

Sleep has become movement;
lip, its understudy.

The Evidence

Ten years gone
the secret is reprised

as mimed truth

decoration above lines

that bone enigma

roughen surface
scarred way back

and the path
stopped up.

Of These

Of these it's the survivors
we attempt to bury:

small discrepancy petrified,
fragment in repetition,
odd assortment of character

once dormant

all materialize
in 'due measure'

as gray corners

blink out

State of Absent

Features no longer clear,
identity enters erasure

(at last)

inverted cone of light
grazes thought,

or its proof.

Account

Urbane target
turns
mustard in hue

again

pictured from
the farther closet,

his story spun

as wreath or ritual.

Melancholy

Honed as
demonstration
the heart strays,

makes adjustments,
closes its volumes

befitting a captious nature

like spray
on walls of its hermitage.

STRANGE PASTURES

Clock

This is not the room.
I am not there.

Unrecognizable.

The face unrecognized
for its calm.

A clock ticks toward
the highest degree of isolation,

a dream on the high slope
whose baffling creatures
go about their ways
ignoring all visitors,

except on occasion
they give that look

it reveals nothing.

Faint Resemblance at a Far Remove
Betrays Distance

1.

Bright beams of replacement flag. Scale pushes through a window which delineates our view. At an oblique angle, shade enters, urging sudden silence, and broad display of day compacts to miscreant's moment gone from focus.

A foreign matter grips like the final with claw, though eventually it burns off to zero gravity, to float through cross-plane havoc.

Remedy will fall then in patterned dust.

The roof provides no adequate vantage point. Caves dotting the hillside don't muffle screams, but instead project them across a span of shared observation, analyzed, in turn, beyond compass of exaction.

Duration divides into random incident.

Motive drowns in tides of upheaval …

Stacks of skewed notion.

2.

Tremor emanates from the source of seclusion something rips at. The intelligible in bondage. Key slipped into crevice.

Apprehension grows; dialogue develops into glossed refraction, with the message coming through as *"notational phantoms,"* whose looks of distress ages can't conciliate. All scorched prodigies of circumstance. Trial in flames.

The delegation experiences decline, while observers at the scene stiffen. Posited belligerence of nature not resting satisfied — and distant.

Overhead, the sound of pacing is heard …

Argument in slow, repetitive motion.

3.

Your metaleptic jottings obscure cause of dissension; land me "belly out in the alcoves." Aspersion in word is recessed there, baroque and "rashly censured." Heteroclite — thorn in sense that plies at remove.

The field of imposture spreads to its furthest boundaries. Moment sinks dead in substance.

"Empty husks that peel off things" litter the scene; produce ambient rustle, which far off vibrates the internals. Nerves quiver in aspic, with no retentiveness but what luck marshals, often in the obverse. Stimulus busied outside the body "besieged by our reasons."

Since "uniformity of posture disposes one to dozing," your keeping me on the fly forces essential abrasiveness to clear the channels — occasionally letting a "furious courier" break loose. Though it seems light years to the margins, taxes the range of device and exhausts natural facility.

Harshness in construction exposes where the effort flags, and sends an organ into eruption. Another mortal part newly stripped. Regret exfoliative in the small round.

Explanation, skimmed from surface, moves in epicycles — then implodes to compressed fruit of stipulation.

Contention dazes. Microscopic shift in observation grows in exertion. Ingenious tack to undergo it all passively.

Recall is "matted all along with winter-green," leaving strong taste at the edges.

4.

Answers are extracted by force applied with an extreme precision — the thick baton landing on the soles of our feet, in measure, along lines of inquiry.

A "Professor of the bastinado" … with grip like ice … still a small digression.

Recondite, his hesitations grow sludge around the ankles.

Our anticipation laden with countermeasure.

5.

Interior voices disagree interminably, sorry conflation of the emblematic
in tow. All because of a spill now splintered at angles, and occluded in
aquamarine. Severally over quotient, condemned to separate a cappella.

True, our questions once had a purity worthy of the Ancients. Clarity
poured from our lips aria-like. But the present leaves only spoils of
intrusion — sleeping idols stretched out in the heat of August.

Alien anxieties rouse old iniquities cribbed in shock, which are counted
forlorn conclusions. Stone-buttocks notations on the sly side, that inspire.

It's like us, to a fault, to make another cadaverous debut ... which from
way back haunt our kind.

6.

Harrowing slices "circumference" through, so what's on edge flies out on dark wings. Messenger-bird as knife; breath in undertow. Your letter, relating events at odds with desire, approaches dimensions too queer for action. Passion agitates ordinary notes, waylaid by "treacherous moon-shine."

Strung out prior to all direction, shapeless elements of sense turn up continually vexed and lacerated. Clouded by an intensification of the blank stare into excess.

So how must we proceed? "Diffusively"? "By starts"? Moving on the words of an actor? Since absence waits in the wings.

"Imperfect translation" is my most immediate response; though it leaves much wanting. We suffer a piracy of the most private areas, listed in opposition, then garbled.

Still, the potential caterpillar within, ravaging energy from what's at hand, gives its soft promise, change at the turn of a season.

7.

Those who confront us are endangered species. Well intentioned, for what they inflict results from fleeing other assailants.

We know them intimately, in dreams, where we see ourselves through their eyes, hear ourselves with their ears.

Suggests a behavior in cycles. Even as lights dim along the horizon.

Quiet meditations, near nightfall, call up cross-bred apparitions of a fall from grace — not the archaic kind — but still make ground dry up and shake.

This season for insomnia urges a correspondence with you, back over decades, even though you've remained near. Just outside the window. Neither gesture nor embrace.

Avian Stroke

1.

It was half-bird, half-man, he observed. Outside, it appeared as bird, while inside, its organs were human. He could tell by the way it moved and would rip at categories until something dripped out and contaminated structure which was its focus …

A tertiary form — "homogeneous on the one side" — whose third element was the spinal fluid it killed for.

2.

Dream of extension moves into the odd register, curves toward "mediate conclusion." And goes flat against the concealed track, "which removes these landmarks" one by one, "preserving only certain monumental aspects."

Now, being accomplice, they will not answer.

3.

The bony ass creature compacts a balmy latitude, with precise description of flora as its disguise. Local delivery of love and hate "whose meaning is *still* not known."

His countenance exhibits "marks of hesitation." Attitude projected as *that dumb look.* The rest being mere transposition, drawing vehemence and pity out.

4.

That "kind of intimation" lodges in the narrows, "separate at last."
The sleepless, who are always watching, contend with "certain tribal
characteristics" *unconditioned and indivisible* ... stepping from shadow.

At the epilogue several are revolted by the injustice — "principle of
aggregation" which unfolds in "all co-operating substances."

Shuffling is heard throughout ever-shrinking quarters. His inquiry takes
another turn "calculated to give a new edge."

5.

Having introduced illusion into its history, he no longer fed inexplicable circumstance. (The tintype wrapped in muslin in order to shield it from light and preserve the few remaining features.)

Fragment intruding into customary avenue of escape.

Or could he devise a way to make his bed burst into flame, then rest assured in a case of mistaken identity ...

Flurry of notice blurs the question. Inherits a new found anonymity — gray being the color of ambient condition.

Studies

1.
Preserved species mowed down, left in mud. Existence by residual.

Uplifted intention separates: Form of solid misbehavior or calculated solitude.

Talking, until dislocated.

Light bends treasure in odd vestments.

2.
Word silted over is left dry and tangent to memory. *(Ephemeral strata.)*

Dawn tightens around the eye. Re-directed climate is investigated many times over.

3.

Unfamiliar sounds stall orientation. Clandestine notice breaks past from present.

Another image is traced: sphere juggled through abandoned street.

Deed misinterpreted, enclaves of broad question are scooped clean.

4.

An unseemly weight on the finger, declamation in tongues, slip through each other like exchanged glances.

Alternative ionizes mind, repels memory.

Wisdom hangs … in vapors.

Biographical Note

Ray Ragosta's previous collections of poetry include *Opposite Ends, Grondines Episode* (both Paradigm Press) and *Varieties of Religious Experience* (Burning Deck).

His work has appeared in *Denver Quarterly, New American Writing, Shiny, Hambone, Aufgabe, Oblek* and other magazines, as well as in the anthologies *One Score More* (Burning Deck), *49+1* (Fondation Royaumont, France) and *A Curious Architecture* (Stride Publications, England).

He lives in Warwick, R.I., and works as a writer and editor.

This book was designed by the author in 10 pt. Palatino, with Optima titles and half-titles, and computer typeset by Rosmarie Waldrop. Printed on 60 lb. Nature's Recycled (an acid-free paper), smyth-sewn and glued into paper covers by McNaughton & Gunn in Saline, Michigan. There are 600 copies.